# More Than I Ever Imagined
## A First-Year Teacher's Discoveries

Nancy Feigenbaum

**Just for Teachers Series**

National Middle School Association
Westerville, Ohio

The materials presented herein are the expressions of the author and do not necessarily represent the policies of NMSA.

NMSA is a registered service mark of National Middle School Association.

Printed in the United States of America.

Betty Edwards, Executive Director
Jeff Ward, Deputy Executive Director
April Tibbles, Director of Publications
Edward Brazee, Editor, Professional Publications
John Lounsbury, Consulting Editor, Professional Publications
Mary Mitchell, Designer, Editorial Assistant
Dawn Williams, Publications Manager
Nikia Reveal, Graphic Designer
Marcia Meade-Hurst, Senior Publications Representative
Peggy Rajala, Publications Marketing/Ad Sales Coordinator

**Library of Congress Cataloging-in-Publication Data**

Feigenbaum, Nancy, 1964-
  More than I ever imagined : a first-year teacher's discoveries / Nancy Feigenbaum.
    p. cm. -- (Just for teachers series)
  Includes bibliographical references.
  ISBN 978-1-56090-216-4
  1. Middle school teaching. 2. First year teachers. I. Title.
LB1735.5.F44 2007
373.11--dc22
                        2007043016

**National Middle School Association**
4151 Executive Parkway, Suite 300
Westerville, Ohio 43081
1-800-528-NMSA   fax: 614-895-4750
**www.nmsa.org**

*Dedication: To my daughters Julia and Elena, who teach me every day*

Thank you to Ed Brazee and National Middle School Association for the opportunity to turn the reflections of my first year into a manuscript that might help others. Ed and Marjorie Artzer are two of many educators who continue to remind me that teaching starts with the students. When I drift too far from this idea—pulled by the enormous demands that all teachers face—my friends and colleagues bring me back. I hope I have succeeded in imparting their spirit to any new teacher who reads this book.

Many ideas in this book were inspired by the work of veteran educators in York County, James City County, and Poquoson, Virginia, who shared their time and creativity, along with the instruction of professors at The College of William and Mary, and Old Dominion University's Career Switcher Program, who helped me make the transition from journalist to teacher. The exceptional staff at Yorktown Middle School have supported me from my first days of full-time teaching. From my start as a Spanish teacher, I had the warm encouragement of the Williamsburg Montessori School, where I first learned to "follow the child."

Any errors in this manuscript are my own. Many improvements came from careful reading by my husband, Bob Evans, and my mother, Lynn Feigenbaum, who have listened to my hopes, worries, and ideas about teaching for years, if not decades.

# Table of Contents

*vii*   **About the Author**

*ix*   **Foreword** by Edward Brazee

*1*   Chapter One
**What Young Adolescents Won't Do**

*6*   Chapter Two
**Before Teaching**

*15*   Chapter Three
**On My Own**

*21*   Chapter Four
**First Days**

*28*   Chapter Five
**Personalities in the Classroom**

*31*   Chapter Six
**Working Too Many Hours**

*39*   Chapter Seven
**How Strict Is Strict Enough?**

*46*   Chapter Eight
**What Young Adolescents Will Do**

*49*   **Postscript**

*53*   **Want to Learn More?**

# About the Author

Nancy Feigenbaum knew she wanted to teach by age four, when she taught the alphabet to a row of cans on her kitchen floor in Puerto Rico, but it took her almost four decades to work up the courage. She took her first detour at Cornell University, earning a degree in Russian literature and Soviet studies. She worked briefly as a travel agent, sending college students on tours of the USSR, before switching to journalism. Writing for daily newspapers in Virginia, North Carolina, and Florida, she found herself daydreaming about the classroom again. At traffic lights between assignments, she scribbled lesson plans into her reporter's notebooks.

Now Nancy teaches Spanish at Yorktown Middle School in Virginia. She has two children (including one in middle school), a husband, and a cat, none of whom she sees as much of as she once did. She has all but given up her hobbies of knitting, kayaking, and playing classical music; but she uses her reporter's notebooks as much as ever—filled now with ideas for her classes.

*Photo by Sangjib Min/Daily Press*

# Foreword

With apologies to a long-forgotten song, teachers could sing, "We get advice, we get advice, we get lots and lots of advice." And they do. Dozens and dozens of books overflow our shelves with every conceivable suggestion for being a successful teacher. This advice runs the gamut from the good, to the bad, and sometimes, the downright silly! *Don't smile until Christmas. Give students something important to do in the first 15 minutes of class. Eat right and get enough exercise. Wear sensible shoes.*

The advice in this interesting book, a part of National Middle School Association's **Just for Teachers** series, won't help you dress more appropriately, but it will give you a lot to think about on the road to becoming a middle school teacher. Nancy Feigenbaum was a successful newspaper reporter for 14 years. Her powers of observation are evident and so is her sense of humor as she describes her first year of teaching young adolescents in a Virginia middle school.

Not surprisingly, Feigenbaum discovers that teaching Spanish to seventh and eighth graders is not exactly what she had envisioned—but along the way she finds that teaching is more than she had hoped. The daily interactions with her students, challenging as they always are, are thoughtfully discussed in the context of her classroom. Every middle level teacher will identify with the situations she describes and learn about becoming a better teacher by listening in as Feigenbaum describes her own trials, challenges, and decisions.

Along the way this first-year teacher at age 41 learns the big lessons that every teacher learns—that teaching is a highly complex mixture of art and science. If it were only "imparting information" or preparing students for the next test—that would be the easy part. The lessons learned here are not gimmicks, or merely a laundry list of quickly forgotten tricks of the trade. Instead of hitting us over the head with prescriptive dos and don'ts, she makes us think critically about the larger issues that underlie teaching—thoughtful and careful planning that connects students to their learning in authentic ways, always keeping the true nature of young adolescents uppermost, responding to students as individuals not only as students, and keeping a sense of humor for the matchless opportunity of working with young adolescents day after day. Who ever said it was going to be easy?

On the surface, this book may appear to be for the beginning middle school teacher. In fact, it is for all teachers. Its lessons—and perhaps more importantly its heart and soul—will resonate with any teacher of young adolescents. I recommend that you reread it at least once every year. Perhaps late February would be a good time for the inspiration that this perceptive teacher offers us to shine through once again.

Nancy Feigenbaum has done every middle level teacher a real service by writing so passionately, thoughtfully, and respectfully about teaching young adolescents and being the absolute best teacher she can be. Read it and enjoy. Read it and learn.

Edward Brazee
University of Maine
September 2007

# Chapter One

# What Young Adolescents Won't Do

## A multiple-choice question for middle school teachers:

Young adolescent boys often refuse to

a. Play hide-and-seek with stuffed animals.
b. Write thank-you notes.
c. Pretend they are Jennifer Lopez.
d. Conjugate verbs.

In most jobs, the biggest dramas of the day come after a few hours. Not for middle school teachers.

In my first year, these dramas met me at the door at 7:55 in the morning. At that hour, I've been known to lose the keys hanging around my neck. If I'm that sleepy, how sleepy are the students pouring into the halls? No time to wonder. The bell has rung, and I'm supposed to be perched at my station, an old wicker stool near the front of the room, where everyone lines up to answer a question about the lesson from the day before, *en español*.

This is where the day's dramas begin. Naturally, the names are changed as I tell you what typically comes next:

Tatiana has been crying, but "it's okay." Emily, who turns out to have attention deficit disorder and stopped taking medication a year ago, skips the line and goes straight to her desk, where she falls into a trance. Miranda is already fiddling with a jar of nail polish. Adam breezes through; he knows the answer and is having an "up" day, so he swaggers to his seat imitating other students. I make a mental note to ask an administrator or counselor about this habit before someone belts him for it.

Then comes Jeremy. Three weeks into this unit, he has no idea how to answer simple questions. Suddenly, I am wide awake.

What happened to all those lessons I've been teaching? The worksheets, the games, the scenes acted out in pairs? Jeremy, a short, quiet boy who often makes As, might as well have been absent.

I happen to teach Spanish. I say "happen to" because surely the same thing happens in math, science, band, and social studies. Anyone who has taught young adolescents has seen this phenomenon: It's a sort of cheerful, quiet strike. Without saying a word, possibly without even thinking a thought, this 12-year-old boy has decided to go no further. He will not learn the next critical skill in the curriculum. His year is over, though he doesn't realize it. It may only be October, but he is already destined to repeat Spanish, or Science 8, or algebra, or whatever.

In Spanish, the standoff moment usually comes with conjugation, the skill of changing verb endings to match the subject of the sentence. It sounds complicated, and it is; but it can't be skipped. People who don't conjugate say things like "You to need pencil. Have one," instead of "I need a pencil. Do you have one?"

Jeremy doesn't care. Here I sit on my wicker stool, facing the reality of my first year of full-time teaching, 38 years after I came home from preschool and "taught" the alphabet to a row of canned beans pulled from my mother's cupboard. The reality is that there are some things young adolescents simply won't do.

As I will see when I grade the next quiz, 18 other students have gone on strike— out of the 120 students taking Spanish I. Another 15 of my Spanish II students didn't learn conjugation last year under the former teacher and still can't do it. What do I do?

I have met more experienced teachers on days like this in the staff room. They look tired and say things like, "They won't do homework." "They won't study." "They don't pay attention." "They won't even put their names on the papers."

They are not exaggerating. There are things middle school students won't do, days they won't learn, moments when they lose what the rest of us call sanity; and all this is normal for a young adolescent.

Not that I knew much about the middle school years just a few months ago. My daughters were then six and ten years old. Before becoming a full-time teacher, I had done a little substituting through the grades, but the Spanish lessons I gave were mostly to elementary school children.

## What it means to be in the "middle"

Now, after a year in a Virginia middle school, I understand vividly what the experts have to say about these contradictory "middle years." For every trait in the books, I can come up with a half dozen faces to match. Take these sentences from "Characteristics of Young Adolescents" in *This We Believe: Successful Schools for Young Adolescents*, a sort of call to arms for middle school educators published by National Middle School Association in 2003. Middle schoolers:

*Undergo bodily changes that may cause awkward, uncoordinated movements.* How many times already have I seen students trip or fall just in the act of entering class? One particularly bright student regularly flew off his chair during otherwise quiet lessons. We joked that his chair was attacking him and stopped paying attention, but the pratfalls continued through the last week of school.

*Have preference for junk food but need good nutrition.* Andrew came to my classroom for lunch every day to play computer games, a privilege that I traded for his cooperation in class. Lunch is a busy time in my room, though, and I don't know how long it took for me to notice that he ate only Slushees and ice cream. The day after I e-mailed his parents, he switched to bagged lunches.

*At times are quick to see flaws in others but slow to acknowledge their own faults.* The girls with the most to learn about tact in my class seemed to be the first to find it lacking in their classmates. I sometimes had to protect students from these self-appointed behavior police. I was fair game, too, of course: "This is no fun." "This class is boring." "You talk too much." "I hate it when you sing." I had to remind myself that while I had to take my students seriously, I didn't have to take everything they said seriously (although these comments often led to improvements in the lessons once I got past the sting).

***Tend to be self-conscious and highly sensitive to personal criticism.*** As a mother of two girls, I was absolutely astonished the first time I made a 13-year-old boy cry. I did it by asking why he didn't have his homework. I made several others cry and turned quite a few more from goofy to sullen before I realized it was better to keep criticism general. "Some people are missing their homework and may lose credit" was a more successful approach, when I remembered to try it.

Girls outwardly seemed less sensitive, but maybe they were just better at disguising their feelings, whether bad or good. More than once, at a ballgame or award night, parents of especially quiet students told me how much their daughters enjoyed Spanish. You could certainly have fooled me!

***Can gravitate toward affiliation with disruptive peers.*** Sometimes, I learned it is easier to predict students' behavior by the people they hang out with than by their own past actions. Annette might not be in trouble yet, but she hangs out with Deidre, and within weeks both have been suspended, a first for Annette.

***Are in transition from moral reasoning that focuses on "what's in it for me" to that which considers the feelings and rights of others.*** Maybe the biggest reason some teachers love middle schoolers—while others consider them the toughest age—is the gap between what they know and what they do. Already they seem so much like adults, able to think abstractly, to empathize, to set priorities. They are confident to the point of cocky. Certainly, they are capable of taking notes, tracking their schedules, outlining reports, meeting deadlines. They have acquired nearly all the tools of an adult, and they demand to be treated as equals. What's more, many of them look an awful lot like adults, towering over me by the age of 12.

So why don't they act more like adults? Why don't they remember their pencils, not to mention their manners? Why are they so sensitive if they are so blunt spoken? Why don't they use their agendas, pace themselves on large projects, show a little kindness in the cafeteria, or any of the million other things they have "learned"? The answers would no doubt fill a textbook on human development.

I had read enough to know I shouldn't be fooled, but it didn't sink in until I had spent a year with my seventh and eighth graders. In fact, the contrast between their deep voices and childish ways sometimes made these young adolescents seem younger still. Did that eighth grader really just wallop the boy in front of him because he didn't move out of the doorway? Yes, despite his honor roll report card, he did. What's more, when confronted, he denied it flatly, as though I hadn't seen the whole quick exchange. Maybe he himself couldn't believe he had done something so stupid.

At my school many gentler souls understand this age and are patient with it. They have tried to show me that this transition to adulthood is part of the curriculum—not part of the problem.

## If the student won't change, the teacher has to

It's one thing to know about the developmental phases of adolescents and quite another to experience them firsthand. I was stunned to have Lisa tell me on Friday that she hated me, but beam at me the following Monday. Though she had been dipping into Ds, she had just earned her first 96 on a quiz.

As a rookie teacher, I also learned that although Shamika is often the first to answer difficult questions, she will spend the rest of her time decorating her notebook and pretending not to pay attention; that Darryl will never say a word voluntarily, but will strut down our makeshift runway for a fashion show; that Ernie isn't listening to a word I say, even though he always has a big smile for me.

These and countless other scenes are the puzzles I have to solve if I am to convince these students to conjugate verbs and make adjectives agree. Eddie and Bill never put their papers in a notebook; as it turns out, they don't even have one for Spanish class. Someone in third period is writing nasty graffiti inside the desk about a beautiful fourth period girl. Ron, Dean, and Tamara each have parents undergoing chemotherapy. Martin likes to wear big pearl necklaces over his T-shirts and his girlfriend's name on his left hand. Many of the girls in my class have decorated their notebooks with their favorite celebrities—half-naked photos of Usher, along with Hello Kitty and Eeyore.

As early as October of my first year, I realized there was no use in getting frustrated with my students when they did things like this (although I still did, naturally). The problem is not what they won't do. Their behavior is so predictable I can look it up in a book. The problem is what I will or won't do.

I won't survive as a teacher if many of my students go on strike for eight out of ten months. Even if my job survived, I wouldn't have the patience for it.

# Chapter Two

# Before Teaching

I started teaching middle school at the age of 41 with that same mixture of terror and exhilaration expressed by nearly all new teachers. I've been told that first-year teachers sometimes get sick on the first day because they are so nervous. I wasn't sick, but it was weeks before I got a full night's sleep as the new Spanish teacher for Yorktown Middle School in southeastern Virginia. I went to bed worrying about lesson plans and woke up dreaming about the classroom. My husband had to apologize to several people after I missed appointments.

What makes these first days so nerve-wracking? It's not just stress. Before teaching, I spent 14 years writing for various daily newspapers, sometimes with less than an hour to report and write the story of a fatal accident. But not even an audience of 400,000 readers made me as nervous as the 27 young adolescents who faced me that first morning in September.

The students were not the problem either. I am not shy around children, and the 700 "Falcons" at Yorktown Middle are an easy bunch to manage, as middle schools go. Our school is set in one of the most historic spots in the United States—students can literally walk a Revolutionary War battlefield—and draws from a long, skinny district of varied neighborhoods. Many of our families are military. A few live in mansions on the Chesapeake Bay, and about as many others live in subsidized apartments. A phone call home solves most problems, though we have our share of front-office regulars.

Drugs, gangs, and teen pregnancy have reached us, of course, but they are still rare enough to get everyone's attention. Typical of middle schools, we have a lot of hallway cliques, and it is important as a teacher not to be seen siding with one over another. Race relations are perhaps our biggest problem as we work to convince African American parents and the small but growing number of Hispanic parents that they can trust us to do our best for their children.

My batch of 160 students turned out to be a fabulous group—funny and bright, if mischievous. However long I teach, I don't think I will ever forget Marc's "non-linguistic representation" for the word *girlfriend*, Samantha's paper-doll T-shirts, or Danika's plywood model house, which appeared spontaneously in class the day everyone else turned theirs in on paper.

Nor will I forget the students who sprouted studs and chains over the course of their 13th year, who brought swastikas into the classroom, who fumed that some new enemy was "in trouble" with them instead of doing my work. They were mine, and I thought about them day and night for ten months. I cried when the buses carried them away on June 15.

## Teacher with a capital T
No, it wasn't the students who worried me as school began. It was the title "teacher." I expected so much from myself as I stood before these children. While they were entrusted to me, I would do everything right, wouldn't I? I would be patient, thoughtful, concerned, well-planned, even entertaining. I would be like the few wonderful teachers I remember from my own childhood, and I would never make the mistakes the worst ones did, or bore the class as the mediocre ones did. The fact that I have made plenty of these mistakes as a parent didn't help me relax my standards as I prepared for the first days of full-time teaching.

Like so many educators, I've known since childhood that I wanted to teach, even that I preferred young adolescents, that most misunderstood and entertaining of age groups. Scarcely more than a teenager myself when I left college, I put off my dream career. I suspected that students would need as much information about life as they would about nouns and verbs, and I simply didn't know enough myself. Twenty years later I decided to stop waiting for wisdom and give it a try.

## Substituting is no substitute for experience, but it's a start
To test the waters, I tried substitute teaching. As people are quick to point out, substitute teaching is entirely different from the daily responsibilities of running a classroom. But it does offer some practical training, along with reducing the

element of surprise for those of us who haven't been in a school for decades. Yes, the girls are wearing blouses *that* deep; and yes, the boys' pants are down to *there*, dress code or no dress code; and yes, both groups will say just what they think about you and your lesson.

As a substitute, I learned how much better students behave once they are called by name. I mastered the 90-name-a-day memorization skill required of subs, a skill more important to a teacher than even typing speed.

Substituting also gave me a chance to practice using my "teacher voice," setting and enforcing rules, and—perhaps the key to succeeding in middle school—keeping students productively busy. In case you should find yourself in the same position, even for a few minutes while a colleague dashes to the front office, here are a few easy classroom games to keep students thinking that served me well:

- *Vocabulary poetry.* Post a list of five to eight key vocabulary words at least six letters long. Each student must choose one vocabulary word, then make a "poem" by writing a related word or phrase using each letter of the vocabulary word.

- *Memory game.* Post a list of vocabulary words on the board to view briefly. Ask a student to step outside, perhaps with a partner. (The classroom is instantly easier to manage if you limit volunteers to those who raise their hands silently. "I would like to choose you, Sam, but I'll have to wait until you're quiet.") Meanwhile, have others help you change the order of the list or add another word. Call the volunteers back to the room and give them ten seconds to guess the change. My favorite part of this game is watching rebellious students "cheat" by writing vocabulary on their arms. Try adding words each round to make the list longer.

- *Hot seat.* Ask for a volunteer to sit in the "hot seat" in front of the room. The volunteer calls on anyone whose hand is raised. The audience is required to try to stump the volunteer with a question about recent material. Students are graded for participation, based on whether they asked an original question (no repeats). The volunteer gets a test grade, a few points of extra credit, or a note of praise to be left for the regular teacher.

  This idea is adapted from the marvelous collection of activities in the book *Foreign Language Teacher's Guide to Active Learning* by Deborah Blaz, and from my observations of veteran foreign language teachers.

- **Family Feud, *classroom style*.** The teacher calls on students who are following class rules (no shouting, moving around, or whatever other behavior needs quelling) to predict the popularity of a movie or song. The student names the item; then the rest of the class guess in writing how many others will agree—as in "13," for "13 students own a copy of this song," or "13 students saw this movie." The class is then surveyed to see if the first student predicted correctly. The game helps force the "all about me" middle schooler to think about other people. Those who are focused entirely on their own habits seldom win.

- ***Add-a-letter word game.*** To prepare, draw a five-by-five grid on a piece of paper, making each of the spaces large enough for a letter of the alphabet. Write a five-letter word across the center line ("t-e-a-c-h"). After that, each player is allowed to add only one letter per turn to form a new word. Words can be read in any direction except diagonal and may twist and turn. However, no squares may count twice in a word and no repeats, plurals, or other similar words are allowed. For example, by adding an "r" under the "a" in "teach," the player forms the word "tear." That student would get four points, one for each letter in the new word.

The day a class full of middle school students missed the dismissal bell because they were so caught up in one of these games, I felt ready for a full-time teaching job.

## Getting organized

I figured that getting organized was the key to succeeding that first year, especially with so many students. By June I knew I would likely have six 45-minute classes a day—an oversized workload of about 160 students that entitled me to an extra stipend but no extra advice. I started to wonder if I had lost my mind starting over with so large a job at an age when most teachers in my school were in a countdown toward retirement.

That first summer I read through my new Spanish textbooks, outlining lessons and project ideas. I interviewed other Spanish teachers, like the reporter I used to be, gratefully copying their best activities and materials. I filled a notebook with what seemed like clever and comprehensive ways to get started.

In my classroom, there would be lots of activities, lots of play, lots of getting up and chatting—in Spanish, of course—and, at the same time, lots of routine and predictability. Young adolescents need that, I'd been told.

When I got my homeroom names—my first class—my ten-year-old daughter helped me memorize them. Long before I met Anne B., I knew she was on the top of my attendance chart, and I could name the other 27 in alphabetical order. Could I have been more ready?

In fact, there were big gaps in my preparation. Grades, for example. Though I had taught Spanish privately for two years, those students were casual about our weekly lessons. They regularly cancelled class and seldom did homework. As a result, I had never maintained a grade book or even given quizzes. I knew a lot about activities, but not assessment. This shortfall was to eat up hours, if not days, of my time as I belatedly learned the value of the advice, "Start with the end in mind."

I also had a queasy feeling about "classroom management," the skill that the quietly effective teacher seems to master intuitively, while the rest of us struggle loudly. I had listened to many lectures and read plenty of well-informed advice, but I still wasn't sure exactly what I would do the day watertight lesson planning wasn't enough. Good thing I didn't know just how waterlogged some of my lesson plans would turn out to be.

Routines are important. I could recite this mantra, but beyond the opening bell-ringer and collecting papers, I had no idea what routines I would need to establish.

Finally, there was the sheer quantity of stuff I was supposed to manage, from student records to the box-loads of materials that came with my textbooks.

## Has anybody seen my chalk?

The single hardest aspect of teaching to explain to people outside education is the volume of the job. During my first year, I found out it wasn't just the 160 students, but the more than 160 sets of parents. For example, I got better results when I called Jason's dad instead of his mother and stepfather. LeeAnne needed a second textbook because she had left her first one at her dad's, and he had become violent. Susan's parents couldn't help her with Spanish when she fell behind, but her stepfather could; he was from Latin America.

It wasn't just lesson plans that needed my attention, but weekly quizzes or tests; and not just the quizzes and tests but the review sheets, and tutoring, and make-ups. The list of make-ups on my board once topped 20 because of an Ecology Club field trip.

What's more, every quiz or test was a sort of inventory that could not be ignored. Each one was like that moment at the door with Jeremy. Why did Ron make a D on this easy weather quiz? (His brother is stationed in Iraq, and Ron is so worried he has developed insomnia.) Isn't this Lisa's fourth low grade in a row? What's going on? (Her parents are divorcing. But this is not the kind of information one gets from a phone call home.) Why did everyone but my language geniuses get numbers 16 and 17 wrong? (I forgot to teach that material after first period.)

Even the small things were sometimes overwhelming. To get through a single lesson I used chalk, whiteboard markers, overhead markers, and a regular pen. I was forever losing these or leaving them on the other side of the room, not to mention overlooking the tests I meant to return or dozens of letters I was expected to hand out as homeroom teacher. Sometimes I felt like I needed a choreographer to decide how I moved around the room during class.

While my colleagues congratulated me on having a wonderful first year, and one even nominated me for the school's "Teacher of the Year Award," I felt as disorganized and out of control as some of my students. Important lists disappeared, e-mails went out of date, and materials were buried. More than once, a last-minute tip from a colleague saved me from embarrassment with the administration. On the last day of school, my students and I came across a wall-sized review puzzle that I could have used a week earlier and now had to store for another year.

Despite all the good wishes to "relax and forget about school" over the summer, I knew I would spend at least part of it making sure I was better organized by fall.

## Watch other people teach

Days before school started, I inherited four file drawers full of paper from the previous Spanish teacher. Among the stacks of tests and worksheets, I found a notebook full of letters home to parents about behavior problems. "Dear _____," they read. The letter that followed was written fill-in-the-blank style. Apparently behavior problems in Spanish class were routine enough to require a form. On some of the quizzes, my predecessor had drawn a line for parents to sign. I began to worry in earnest.

Would I be writing form letters home because I had so many discipline problems? Would it take a parent's signature to make sure students did well on quizzes? This was not the kind of teaching I had been dreaming about for decades. I remember being disgusted back in high school by teachers who spent all their time trying to get the class quiet. None of us learned anything—at least, not from them. Those of us who cared went home and read the book. What happened to the rest of the students?

I had witnessed many learning atmospheres working as a substitute. Usually I was alone in class when I substituted, but now and then I took a job as an aide and got to see other teachers at work. These experiences were very revealing.

- One class of high school students maintained silence as the teacher delivered a well-crafted, 30-minute history lecture. The teacher kept strict control and publicly admonished the few who crossed the line. The students also took a quiz on Russian geography, which I would have flunked, despite being a Soviet studies major in college (many of them did flunk, in fact).

- In a tiny, remedial high school math class, the teacher gave students the day off, saying that sometimes they simply needed a break.

- In a high school across town, there was plenty of chatter in a class of college-bound students whose parents came from lower income backgrounds. Small groups of students worked and gossiped in turn as they plowed through advanced math and science with the help of tutors. One student came in swaggering because she had been chosen to present a problem in front of the math class that day.

- In one high school civics class, the teacher was giving a quiz for the second time because the students had done so poorly. To prepare them, he reviewed all the questions on an overhead. Most of the class talked through his presentation as he warned them they would flunk again.

Finally, I will never forget the English class where students sat in groups with worksheets about a classic piece of American literature they were reading. I don't remember seeing the teacher emerge from her desk once until the end of the 90-minute period. Then she made a comment something like this: "Please remember that if you have questions, you can come up and ask them. I have read all these books that I assign to you—although I haven't read some of them for a while." (Ten years is the figure that sticks in my mind.) At this point, a student at my table had a question about the plot line. Had the character's wife lived or died after her illness? The teacher answered it incorrectly.

Here are some lessons I learned about organization in my first year:

- Have a set place for important papers so they don't wind up in the big stack where they would be lost until the end-of-school filing spree. For me, that turned out to be a different colored folder for each period, a plain folder for make-up quizzes, and a clipboard for seating charts.

- Have a place for the other papers, too, if possible. Setting aside a few hours early in the year to create a filing system would have saved me days of work later.

- Every time you assign a project, consider its final destination. Will it hang on the wall? Go home with students? Be included in their portfolios? Go straight to the trash? Don't forget to keep a few of the finest for your records and examples for next year's lesson.

- Keep a master copy of all quizzes and tests in a separate file. Even if you don't offer retakes, as I did, you'll need them for the students who need tutoring or extra help.

- Find out what's on the calendar. More than once, I laid out an entire week of lesson plans before realizing there was a spirit rally, a testing day, or report card coming up. Often, this information was buried in a stack of e-mails I had read too quickly or in a public file other teachers checked but I didn't know existed.

## Quietly great teaching

Much better were the days when I asked the students and faculty to recommend their favorite instructors. During my substitute planning hour or on a separate day, I saw several terrific teachers at work. They were all very different, but a few constants stood out:

- My first impression was that these teachers were unimpressive. They did not seem especially charismatic or entertaining. They weren't like rock stars at a concert, with teenagers competing for their attention. Students followed their lead but focused mainly on one another, working in pairs or watching those already called to the front of the room.

- The teachers were nearly constantly focused on the students. They led activities, sparked discussion on an overhead, strolled around checking pairs' progress on an oral exercise. They moved the class from one activity to the next smoothly, without any scolding or sarcasm—with hardly any comment about students' behavior, in fact.

- These classes weren't perfect, of course, but disruptions were exceptional and ended quickly. The few students with obvious behavior problems acted out at regular intervals, but lacking an audience, their outbursts blew over quickly. I watched one fidgety boy get out of his chair repeatedly in a middle school class without attracting attention. The teacher later explained that she knew he had trouble sitting still and let him stand as long as he stayed close to his seat.

- It's also worth noting that the lessons I watched weren't particularly showy. The materials themselves weren't complicated or technically difficult to produce. One teacher used handwritten handouts for a project guide (and his handwriting wasn't particularly neat). Another let students create their own bingo games. She had them act out a charades game in pairs. A frail teacher with the reputation of a master assigned project after project that focused on the children's own lives with nothing more than poster board, paper, pencil, and a little fabric. The students did not seem to notice that she had been fighting an illness all year.

- All of these teachers shifted activities and learning styles often, even as they stuck to a theme. If the subject was how to phrase commands, the students might be at the board, then playing bingo, then chatting in pairs, then playing charades—all the while learning to say commands.

These were the teachers who, as a friend puts it, are interested in learning—their own as well as their students'. Could I be like them?

## Chapter Three

# On My Own

It was a good thing I had watched other teachers when I had the chance. Once I started teaching full-time, there was hardly time to leave the room for lunch, much less visit another classroom, because of the overload I taught. Other teachers were encouraged to observe one another during their duty period.

The isolation of teaching was one of the surprises of that first year. How can anyone be alone amid so many people? I was the only Spanish teacher that year, and some days I was the only foreign language teacher in the building. My peers in the so-called department taught physical education, art, and keyboarding; my school mentor was an expert in math. We might as well have been speaking different languages—in fact, we were—oral assessments versus Presidential Fitness Awards, binomials versus reflexive verbs. My university mentor—a retired Spanish teacher and professor—was my main connection to the field I taught, and I was always grateful for her visits.

The principal weighed in on my lesson plans occasionally, and the assistant principal was generous with his time in a crisis. But mostly, I felt breezily and scarily on my own.

I had forgotten a page out of Harry Wong's classic *The First Days of School* about teacher isolation. Wong writes, "Teacher isolation is a reality." He doesn't get into details, but I was living them.

I worked alone most days, while most other teachers worked in pairs or departments. That meant they had the burden of cooperating when their teaching styles might be different, but it also meant they could rely on one another. I made up all my own quizzes and tests and sometimes entire units of curriculum.

Some days I felt like a stay-at-home mom with 160 children, not to mention the hundreds of sixth graders who shared the hallway. I found excuses to go to the library or counselor's office during my precious planning time—so that I could speak to an adult.

## Freedom to take risks

Of course, there were advantages to being so alone. No one tried to talk me out of trying the crazy ideas I'd read about or invented, which ranged from playing Go Fish in Spanish to creating human calendars (in the latter game, each student wears a day-of-the-week sign, and a volunteer positions classmates in the right order). I brought in boxes of Alpha-Bits to practice the Spanish alphabet, only to find more bits than letters. (It turns out there are whole Web sites on classroom lessons built around Alpha-Bits, including one at Technospud.com, which involves estimation and averaging. Thanks to the Internet, it seems, no teacher is completely alone.)

The mix-and-match department to which I belonged gave me an early taste for collaboration—a practice that is soon to become the rule at my school and many others. Between us, the teen-living teacher and I worked out a classroom swap so my students could open a "restaurant" and practice ordering food and acting the role of waiters. The art teacher often lent me supplies. When I mentioned a daydream about using Latino percussion instruments to help with memorization, the band teacher promptly came up with a supplier and a list of prices. The keyboarding teacher loaned us her cameras so we could personalize the dull and difficult work of irregular verbs.

The Spanish students and I were on our own, however, the day of our fashion show, complete with pink floor lights and emcees. No administrator happened to walk in on "flying-animal conjugation day," either, so I never learned if it crossed a line into chaos. (Every time students launched an animal, they had to declare the fact in Spanish, then describe who had the animal next.)

I was also on my own the day the students used the digital cameras to "direct" scenes for their project on the challenging preterite tense. When I printed out the photos, I discovered that several featured pieces of paper rolled up to look like cigarettes and soda bottles that had morphed into beer bottles. Those didn't go on the display board.

I wound up receiving my best advice from my university-assigned mentor and my school mentor, the award-winning math teacher. No book in the world can offer what one veteran can. My school mentor had only to sit in on two of my classes before discipline was tightened considerably.

But for all the great advice about reflecting on lessons and seeking help, the first year of teaching may simply be too busy for such luxuries. Sometimes sitting down and talking to my school mentor meant staying up another hour past my bedtime grading quizzes. She herself was working long hours even before I was added to her copious responsibilities. And one thing I already knew for certain about this job: It's not one to be done while exhausted.

## On-the-job training

Especially frustrating during those first few weeks were days of orientation and professional development that went over my head, while I still lacked the basics. One of the most memorable was a lecture from a stern veteran aimed at brand-new teachers like me: "Put your clothes out the night before," she commanded. That and "never e-mail an angry parent" are among the few pieces of advice I could remember after the first bell rang.

For the rest, I knew mainly that plenty of advice existed; and if I needed some, I'd better find an expert. My notes from the new teacher orientation are full of scribbles and a few minor tips like these—hardly the advice on which to launch a career:

- Never send an e-mail to everyone in the school system.

- Close your door when running the air conditioner.

- Only the principal can reset your computer password.

- At retirement, you can collect $30 for sick leave you didn't use, up to 100 days. (Sick days? I didn't dare use them unless I was running a fever. I knew how little students learned from substitutes.)

# What I wish I had been told

- Attendance is sacred. It overrules everything else, including lesson plans and minor medical emergencies, so find a way to take it on time. Also, never file away an absence note from a parent. The front office may never forgive you.

- Find out what else is sacred. In our school it's the list of who gets which textbook and whether textbooks were returned. Also critical are records of parent contacts, locker numbers, and the green sheet of paper every teacher carries during fire drills to signal "everybody's here."

- Each school seems to have its own culture. Ours puts a big emphasis on caring for individual students, which means that even a teacher with 160 of them is expected to call home after a failed test. One weekend I had to call dozens of parents.

- Teach the habits that matter most to you. I never pursued the chewing gum bandits, but by the end of the year I was still giving students lessons in cleaning out their desks and pushing in their chairs. I also wish I had made it clear early in the year that the small sarcasms and put-downs common among today's teenagers were not allowed in my class. A few students who started off making wisecracks had turned unruly by January.

- Learn everyone's name, especially the front office staff, the maintenance staff, and the boys with identical haircuts. Do whatever it takes to learn these names, and do it early. Geneva was "Geneva from Geneva, Switzerland" all year, and she didn't mind it nearly as much as being confused with Genny. For a while I set aside the first few minutes of each class for practicing names. The students especially liked it when I let them quiz and grade me.

- Learn the traditions and requirements. This includes the midterm exam that is required for all high school credit classes, but which I didn't realize I was supposed to give. Later, I was also surprised to learn I would have to analyze and relate the test questions to the units studied and the state's Standards of Learning. I scrambled to work backwards for information I should have collected first. Other exams had a big effect on my class, too, not only distracting students but sapping their focus. After Virginia's enormously important Standards of Learning examinations in May, students openly confessed that they were "done." The following year I had those dates on my calendar and knew to spice up my lessons accordingly.

- Get students involved. I could feel teacher burnout starting early when I found myself working on bulletin boards late into a 60-hour week. By the end of the year, students were vying to climb the stepladder to do this work, and much more. On the best days, the classroom was truly theirs. These were the days when the routines and discipline I had set up worked well enough that I could set students loose to learn all they could on their own. Any failure of the first element, however, meant I could not afford the second; and these golden days were precious. One of my favorite memories was the day *after* biographical posters were due. In a last-minute flash of inspiration, I ditched my lesson plan and instead assigned students to wander the halls that were plastered with their work. Carrying whiteboards and markers, they were to agree or disagree with their classmates' comments—all in Spanish, and all using some of the toughest vocabulary in the chapter. No one had trouble with this material on the final exam.

- For large numbers of supplies, consider asking your students. Asking every child to bring in two envelopes got me the 160 I needed for one of my activities (about half the students forgot theirs). Parents were good about donations early in the year, but by the fourth quarter their responses fell way off (see next item).

- Assume students will forget. Unless you want to spend the first year arguing with 13-year-olds, assume they will forget pencils, paper, textbooks, and the whiteboard markers you absolutely insisted are required for class. Find the easiest way possible to deal with this shortage (for example, you can ask students to bring in spare whiteboard markers at the beginning of the year to loan out), so that your class time is dedicated more to learning than lecturing.

One of the best pieces of advice I got was to give up the battle over pencils. Plenty of teachers still take money or collateral for loaning these, but I was busy trying to work out my first year's lessons. Instead, I collected the grungy stubs I found around school and gave these out for the chronically forgetful.

Forty-five minutes is simply too little time to squander on these meaningless tug-of-wars. I can hardly keep track of my own pens, so how can I expect it of a younger person who switches classes seven times a day and just got hauled into the principal's office for a food fight? On the other hand, middle school may be the perfect place to gently teach better organizational skills, without an embarrassing lecture. No doubt there are more experienced teachers doing this successfully.

–   Listen carefully at the water cooler. The emphasis here is on "carefully." New teachers are often warned to avoid the complainers in the teachers' lounge. Yet it was there that I learned one of my students thought she was pregnant; that another had an addict for a parent who was frequently absent from home; that a third had run away, not simply visited her grandparents, as the parents explained. There was vague suspicion that a fourth student might have been beaten after teachers called home about his misbehavior. While I should have been treating everyone with the greatest tenderness and concern, I made sure it was true of these four who needed it most.

# Chapter Four

# First Days

**P**eople watching me get ready must have thought I was a little crazy that first week of school. They would have been right.

First came the shock of seeing the Spanish classroom in its bare state. With a renovation looming in 18 months, nothing at Yorktown Middle School was going to be replaced or replastered if it could hang on long enough to be gutted. The room I was assigned had been a lovely special needs facility the year before. Stripped of all the previous teacher's creativity, I saw it for what it was: an old science classroom whose cinder block walls and blackboards were pockmarked with bits of dried putty and double-sided tape that never did come off.

The ancient heater/air-conditioner was original to the building of the school and gave a rattle like my Dad's old VW Beetle whenever it came on—not an asset to a class based on listening and repeating. Fortunately, a neighboring colleague who'd had the room a decade earlier showed me how to turn it off with a flathead screwdriver, although we never could get the decades of dirt out of the grill.

Inexplicably, a map in French hung on the wall. The French room had none. And it would be weeks before I had a computer, despite the daily reminders from the front office to take attendance online.

I wanted the students' desks to face me in shallow, semicircular rows, like a small amphitheater. For this plan, the overhead faced the wrong way, and the big TV screen, when it arrived, would be at their backs; so I decided that the students could turn around to watch movies, and I brought in a white sheet to serve as a makeshift overhead screen, tacked up over the chalkboard. Then I ditched elaborate plans for painting a map of Spain and Latin America, and went to town with the colored paper rolls I discovered at the farthest end of the school (I got lots of exercise that first week). By the first day of school, the room was bright with reds and yellows—nothing subtle, I have no talent for art—with black lettering spelling the name of each Spanish-speaking country.

Nine huge posters I had begged from tourism agencies hung tenuously from the cinder block. These would come down, one at a time, throughout the year, every time we opened our unscreened windows to let in cooler air—and wasps. (Forget terrorist emergency plans. Every teacher should have a wasp emergency plan so as not to lose 30 minutes to giddy, hysterical 13-year-olds.)

But no matter, the room was starting to look like a Spanish class instead of a therapy room or, worse, a class where it was permissible to speak English. Nothing in English was to be seen except the evacuation procedure sign. Even the DARE sticker donated later by a policeman was in Spanish.

Incidentally, the putty I used to hang the posters, the posters themselves, the Spanish language map I brought out for geography lessons—I supplied all of these. The school was helpful whenever possible, presenting all new teachers with a small basket of supplies, from a stapler to a box of individual erasers (I wouldn't understand the purpose of the latter until I gave my first fill-in-the-bubble-in-pencil test). Later, the front office bought 27 pairs of scissors, seven Spanish-English dictionaries, and 20 novels at my request; but in the hectic days before school started there was no time. Getting ready turned out to be my responsibility.

I brought in my wicker stool, laid out the well-organized files that would turn out to be completely inadequate, and was as ready as I knew how to be for my first students.

## The roller coaster takes off

What I remember from those first days feels like it was filmed at double speed—fascinating, exciting, and too fast to sort out. The students came, worked, and left before I could take stock. At first, I kept notes on each class—"Period 5 never got to the pairs exercise," "Laticia and James are talking too much in English"—but the five-minute transitions proved too short for anything but the search for whiteboard marker, chalk, and the next list of names. One class went well, the next was almost a disaster; and I was too busy, mercifully, to worry too much.

It would take me weeks, even months, to sort everyone out—not just in terms of names but in terms of which small, quiet girl was the straight-A seventh grader and which was the skateboarder with the plummeting grades. Thank goodness for the much-vaunted "honeymoon" of the first semester. I had to split up a budding white supremacist from the pair of African American girls he was taunting; another pair had to be reseated when the flirting turned to anger; but otherwise I don't remember any major discipline problems.

For the most part, the students were happy with the pace of instruction. True to my goal, classes were generally active, light, and focused on the students themselves. In this respect, foreign language teachers are uniquely lucky. As I tell my students, Spanish I is the only class where you get As for talking about yourself.

Grades at this point were high, and most students came along pretty successfully. Of course, some slipped past me unnoticed. Even for a new teacher, I felt painfully clueless. Maybe this was partly because I'd had another career and knew what it was like to become competent at a job. As a journalist, I had been tapped for management and told I had a bright future—before I decided that future didn't appeal to me.

Starting over as a teacher offered me the humbling, if exciting, chance to feel completely ignorant again, only this time with a better idea of what was at stake. I now know that during those first weeks my eyes had not yet acquired "teacher sight," an ability to focus one's attention exactly where it's needed and screen out the rest. Just a few months later, I began to pick up on the joyful hum of a busy class, to relax enough to pick out which students weren't in the flow.

By March, I could list the students who consistently turned things in late, which C averages reflected too many Ds, whose absences were truly alarming, or which students were afraid to go home with a discipline note. Speaking to one parent too late in the year about her child's sinking grades, I could only apologize. Why hadn't I seen the pattern in October? I couldn't give a reasonable excuse. I was simply too overwhelmed and inexperienced to pick up on it.

## Old habits die hard

The classes that went well those first weeks benefited from the novelty factor. Unlike math and English, Spanish was a subject most of my students had never taken before. When I asked students to stand in front of the class and pretend to be Jennifer Lopez or Santa Claus, they accepted the assignment with surprisingly little hesitation. They eagerly competed in whiteboard dictation races, drew goofy cartoons, and wrote letters to "secret" buddies in other classes, not knowing there was any other way to learn this different subject.

Occasionally we crossed the line into teenager mortification—chanting aloud or pointing to the furniture we were naming or responding to my weird stories. At those times, I warned those who were too cool to take part that they'd be doing it alone, in front of all of us, if they didn't join in. But I didn't tread there too often. I didn't make the carefully dressed girls, some of them looking like runway models, stand in front of the class to present their projects. They didn't really want the attention they seemed to be asking for. Eventually, I learned that these same girls did fine if I had everyone make presentations in the four corners of the room.

My small Spanish II classes were another story. Accustomed to another teacher's methodology, these two classes were much less willing to take chances with me. Nearly everything I did right in Spanish I seemed to go wrong with Spanish II. Active lessons set off misbehavior. Quieter lessons set off chatter and boredom. These students started the year by talking too much in English and ended the year much the same way. I lost my temper, lectured, and warned, without any improvement, of course. They were used to doing things a certain way, and I had no idea how to change it.

I have since heard a couple of disaster stories about teachers coming into high school Spanish programs where they were supposed to clean things up but instead struggled with the classes they inherited. Parents and students are fairly harsh about these teachers' lack of control. I am less judgmental after my own first year.

My first days of teaching were certainly better for the professional education books I had to read. I think those aimed at rank beginners are some of the most helpful. One veteran teacher told me he rereads Wong's *The First Days of School: How to Be an Effective Teacher* twice a year to stay fresh.

## Survival skills

Here is a sampling of the tips that helped me the most in setting the right tone and surviving:

- **Teach something the first day.** Some new teacher books advise against rushing into lessons, but I preferred the advice I got from a retired educator: to give students on the first day a skill to show off. After introductions and paperwork were out of the way, they learned a single phrase and tried it out on one another. They left feeling powerful, excited to crack the code of a foreign language.

- *Keep it light.* My private joke was, "It's only Spanish class," and while I never shared it with the students, I constantly tried to remind myself that it was true. The less seriously I took things, the better the students seemed to do. Even the most fortunate students often had bigger problems than fulfilling the day's academic objective. One day when my students were clearly exhausted, we tossed out the lesson plan and switched to a team competition. On any day, students too angry or upset to work got a pass to the bathroom.

- *Make your home life as easy as possible.* That means no out-of-town trips, elaborate gatherings, or extra sports for the children who have to be ferried around after work.

- *Say hello.* This advice might sound too obvious, yet it is easily overlooked. When you're busy with problems from the last class, you might ignore students coming in for the next one. With less than five minutes of transition time, I was often frazzled or scrambling for notes, but I did manage to greet students at my door with a question almost every day of class.

- *Be fair.* While students were responsible for the work, the responsibility for teaching was mine. I would not deliberately test them on anything I had not taught. I would not ask the impossible of them, or even the unlikely. More than once, I accidentally wrote quizzes that were too hard. If I realized it in time, I reminded the class that I would eliminate unreasonable questions (based on most students' getting them wrong). When I had to present a stack of bad grades, a pep talk beforehand and an offer to retake the quiz or drop the lowest grade ensured that my students would keep learning rather than sulking.

- *Encourage, encourage, encourage.* People seem to have a special anxiety about learning foreign languages, although other teachers may say the same about math, English, or hitting a volleyball. I wanted students to believe they could learn this subject and have fun doing it. Even parents and fellow teachers needed encouragement. Everyone seemed to have a story about taking four years of Spanish or French and forgetting it all. Bluffing a certain amount, I told them it would be different for their children and why (this is where all the classroom jargon came in handy; things have changed since most adults went to school and sat at a desk hour after hour). This is a lesson I forgot by the end of the year, I confess. I'm still embarrassed by the lectures I gave lagging students in May.

- *Be up front with your expectations and rules.* I fell short here, not being sure what I would need. The next year, for example, I added an up-to-date notebook of classwork and homework to the requirements. But I was bold enough my first year to declare that there would be nightly homework. There would be homework on test nights and Friday nights, even during hurricanes, I said (exaggeration seems to take the sting off bad news). This rule worked so well that when I forgot to distribute assigned handouts, many students brought in other work.

- *Enforce your rules.* I've since learned that students will go along with almost any rule, provided the teacher goes along with it. In other words, if I tell students I expect them to have notebooks, I must grade them. Otherwise my so-called requirement is nothing but a suggestion. The biggest expectation I had was the most obvious and perhaps the most inflated: that students would always pay attention. Chatting, drawing textbook graffiti, painting fingernails with permanent markers, flipping tiny plastic skateboards, and performing surgery on broken mechanical pencils—these were never in my idealized daydreams of teaching. Nevertheless, I saw all of these before 9 a.m. most days. My homeroom students were noisy and quick to "finish" work, so they could go back to discussing last night's football game or drawing anime characters. Veteran teachers don't seem to have this problem. If quiet is what they want, they get it, starting first thing in the morning. For me, it still takes a period or two to lay down the law.

- *Decide how students will come and go from class.* Will you need printed passes? A wooden hall pass for the restroom? A check-out notebook? I hate dealing with these kinds of housekeeping details, and as a result, I have more interruptions cutting into instruction time than most teachers.

- *Hold students accountable from the start.* During my first year, students who forgot homework were quietly handed a laminated yellow card to copy (in Spanish, but with an English translation in small print): "I don't have my homework. It is my responsibility. Signed, _____." I promised that if these piled up they would be presented to parents as evidence, though I never had to. Students knew I had the letters and didn't lie when confronted. Thanks to my sister-in-law Annie Evans (whose classroom management is legendary in nearby Henrico County) for this tip. During my second year of teaching, the school system instituted an almost identical program.

– *Be as humane as possible, even when you think it's not necessary.* Despite my draconian homework policy, I kept assignments very short and allowed two freebies every nine weeks. Few students needed more, and the free days were a great relief to the emotional, high-achieving students who, like everyone else, had a bad day now and then. Knowing that many students would lose homework assignments, I told them they could submit anything written with the most recent vocabulary. Whenever I saw a lot of this in class, it usually meant I had made the assignment too difficult.

Looking back at my own advice, I see the themes from *This We Believe*, National Middle School Association's statement about teaching to this age group. To get through to middle school students, I have to reach them as individuals yet understand them as a group. My class may count as high school credit, and the material is sometimes elementary, but the students who face me every day are young adolescents. Every lesson I write must pass this reality first. Otherwise, my students will pull out their headsets or their toy skateboards and tune out, and I will wind up at the water cooler complaining about what middle school students won't do.

# Chapter Five

# Personalities in the Classroom

I read quite a bit about classroom management before I entered the classroom. There was a lot of helpful advice, much of which I would not truly understand for at least a year. However, nothing I read prepared me for one of the key realities of teaching: coping with so many personalities. At home, we are four people and a cat, maybe 15 at family gatherings. At my last job, I had to get used to a close circle of about six people, plus another dozen when working outside the department. In teaching, without even counting my colleagues, I have hundreds of people to get along with and get to know.

When I started last year, I had no idea what this reality would entail. I imagined that I would have to stay aloof from students, with such a large group. I was frustrated that I had so little time to get to know them. Soon after school started, I found myself putting them in categories—which ones worked hard, which seemed particularly intelligent, which consistently scored lower than they ought to have.

There were categories I hadn't anticipated, too—under- and overmedicated students, students falling in love or coping with breakups, students with mild speech defects or some unnamed problem hearing the Spanish accent, students motivated only by sports, students who didn't sleep enough, students who never—absolutely never—remembered a pencil or put away a piece of work in their binders.

# Growing and changing

Soon after December, though, I began to see differences in the people I was getting to know. Leah had begun the year hardworking but struggling. She came in at lunchtime for help, confessing that she had never willingly read a book and had to study hard for some classes. Sometimes she made Ds in mine. Then, something changed. After a few tutoring sessions, she began getting Cs and Bs, then low As. One day in March, I handed her back a quiz with a "100%" on the top. "Are you sure this is my paper?" she asked. "Oh, yes," I replied, "and one of the few 100s on this quiz." I never had to worry about Leah's progress afterward.

About the same time, her best friend Rosie sank from Cs and Ds to Fs. She came in for help occasionally, always at the last minute, and talked longingly about getting good grades, but didn't study. Even at tutoring she happily chatted rather than studied. By the end of the year she was making Ds in nearly every class, and her parents were beside themselves.

Other changes were taking place in my classroom, too, as the year went on. Adam, who started off with a sharp tongue but a generally cooperative attitude was generating talk in the teachers' lounge by April. He was quick with putdowns and sighs, got out of his chair for no reason, and forever distracted the people around him while ignoring his own work. His first-semester A fell to a C. One week he set a class record, bringing in one piece of homework out of five and demanding congratulations when he did. The more attention his outbursts attracted, the worse they became, ending with an accusation that was becoming familiar from other troublemakers: "How come I'm the only one who gets in trouble?"

I had no solutions for Adam, so I backed off as much as possible publicly and talked to him in the hall when necessary. In June, I sent him on his way with a silent wish for some growing up over summer and concern for his next teacher.

What about Justine, who could not meet my eyes for the first few weeks of school? Small and shy, she did not find school easy. Sometime in November, she decided I was trustworthy and began looking me in the eye. After that, her neat work, often decorated in color, was so free of errors it made me feel my assignments were too easy. Why she did so well in my class and not others, I have no idea. We never had a real conversation. I can't claim any special rapport with her.

Of course, for every Justine there was a Shamika, clearly one of my brightest and most attentive students at the beginning of the year. By the end, I was the only teacher battling her for control of the classroom. Again, I have no idea why, and

I didn't see it coming. I can only say that with Shamika small missteps had big consequences, and by May it was so bad we shocked each other by having a full-blown, yelling argument. This was so far from my ideals that I was upset for days. Talking to other teachers not only didn't help much but felt humiliating, since they clearly weren't having as much trouble with her.

A sentence in *This We Believe* strikes me as a key to the answer:

"Young people undergo more rapid and profound personal changes between the ages 10 and 15 than at any other time in their lives."

Infants grow physically as much as young adolescents, but they are lucky enough not to be conscious of these changes, and they do not face the social and emotional changes that 10- to 15-year-olds do.

I would add that these changes will play out differently for students like Shamika, Adam, and Rosie because their backgrounds are so different. One comes from an upper middle class family where college is considered standard. Another comes from a middle class home that has never seen a child with so little interest in schooling. A third comes from a proud, self-conscious family working hard for financial stability.

It's not enough to know that middle schoolers go through incredible changes, or that they come from radically different homes. It will take years of putting these factors together to learn the different approaches people require at this age.

In my final evaluation, the principal suggested I focus the following year on using more technology in my classroom. Technology happens to fit nicely with my curriculum, so it was easy to oblige; but with all due respect, I disagree about whether this was really my biggest challenge. It was the changes I saw in Shamika, Adam, Rosie, and others that had my full attention as I got ready to start the next year.

## Chapter Six

# Working Too Many Hours

I have been lucky so far not to run into anyone who heard me say a year ago, "I'm not going to work late." I did get home most days at a decent hour, if by decent I mean dinnertime. But at 41, I was working 10- to 12-hour days plus weekends for the first time in my life. The custodians were often the only people in the building by the time I left: "Don't you like your family?" one of them finally asked in May, when the long days had not slackened. Another guessed: "You don't know how to cook, do you?"

By then I felt especially lucky to have a husband who had willingly taken over not only the cooking but dishes, laundry, and checkbook. I believe that handoff saved us a fair amount of money in late fees, not to mention our marriage. "First-year teacher's husband" is a term I hadn't heard until then, but I certainly understood it. When you're working this hard just to get through the day, you need a very understanding spouse.

Now that I've finished my first year of full-time teaching I have tried to figure out exactly what soaked up so much time. I usually arrived earlier than most teachers—between 7 and 7:20 a.m. for a schedule that started by 8. The buses left at 2:45 p.m. All teachers got 45 minutes of planning time, along with a duty period that most new teachers spent grading papers. I taught an extra class during that time, which not only boosted my pay more than ten percent but exempted me from monitoring the hallways or cafeteria.

If I left by 5:40 p.m., in time to eat with the family, I could work another three hours. Surely that was enough planning and grading time. Yet nearly anyone who has taught will not be surprised when I say that it wasn't. There were still many nights when I sat at the kitchen table grading papers, and weekends when I put in ten hours more on work.

My husband comes from a family of teachers, so they understood when I missed family get-togethers. My sister-in-law still works many late nights after 19 years on the job, as do a few of the veteran teachers at my school (a fact that worries me, I'll admit).

But I am the first on my side of the family to teach children, and my relatives plainly thought I was a little possessed. We would plan a trip to visit my mother, and I would bring a sack full of papers or a lotto game to sketch out. Even other teachers tried to get me to leave as they walked out the door at 4 p.m., forgetting, maybe, how much they rely on the work and experience they have built up over a career. My assistant principal never rushed me out of the building. I think he understood I needed a few hours of quiet to be ready for the next day's clamor. Six hours of bad lessons feels a lot longer than a longer day that hums.

Even with the extra hours not everything got done. For example, all that helpful extra reading suggested by the principal—I fell behind at about month three. Professional journals? Notes I had taken? All ignored until summer. I assigned journal writing that I had no time to grade. The weekly grading got done quickly, but make-up work piled up for weeks. Planning was similarly dicey. There were black holes in my calendar where projects should have been. Thank goodness our copy machines (nearly) always worked, allowing me to indulge in last-minute brainstorming.

Effective foreign language teaching relies heavily on "manipulatives"—things students can hold in their hands. I managed to introduce quite a few of these in our routines, but I think the students could have used twice as many.

I guess that I put in 20 to 35 hours a week on top of classroom instruction time my first year, counting planning periods, late afternoons, evenings, and weekends. Sixty-hour weeks were not uncommon.

## Where did the time go?

So, where did all that time go, and—now I wonder—how can I do things differently to have a bit of my private life back? The simple answer is preparing lessons. Sometimes it felt as though I worked two hours for every one I taught. Here is a more detailed breakdown:

***Extra work hours.*** My school strongly encourages (I think "requires" wouldn't be a stretch) teachers to offer tutoring once a week. Students come to class starting at 2:37 p.m. and stay until the late buses leave at 4 p.m. Tutoring days were exceptionally tiring, and I found it hard to get much done afterward. Teachers are also asked to sponsor clubs that meet every week or two. The foreign language club had to share my attention with everything else.

We had staff meetings nearly every Monday. These were important sources of information and interaction with other teachers, especially for a novice like me.

Incidentally, I also had Girl Scout troop meetings to lead every other week. Here is where the balance of home and work gets tricky. It seemed ridiculous to continue with Girl Scouts once I started teaching, but no other mom would take over because no one felt prepared to manage a troop of young adolescent girls.

Picture a typical after-school schedule:

Monday: Staff meeting
Wednesday: Foreign language club or Girl Scout meeting
Thursday: Tutoring
Friday: Entering the week's grades and attendance in the computer

Only on Tuesdays was I free to sit at my desk directly after the last class.

***Lesson planning.*** Within months of starting my job, I realized that lesson planning was not a one-time but a two- or even three-time process. I am a little hesitant to admit this, but I suspect if I do, many of my colleagues will say they had the same problem their first year. First came the lessons I was required to submit in advance for my principal—correlated to state Standards of Learning and (on a good week) the effective teaching strategies we were learning as a faculty. Written after school in about an hour and a half, these were often sensible but not terribly exciting, or, on the flip side, exciting but wildly impractical.

I almost never taught from these lesson plans, but they were useful as a first step in thinking about the week—almost like a rough draft for a writer. Just as useful was a page I added on my own, "this week vs. last week," where I listed what I had just taught and what I hoped to teach next. I consulted this list throughout the week to stay on track.

Next came the lesson plans I rewrote a night or two before, or even that morning, as I realized where my teaching was actually headed or came up with more creative or truly effective ideas for class. Often, it was in the morning shower that I realized my students needed some conversation practice, not writing time, or were overdue for a review of numbers or … some other "brilliant" idea. No wonder I was one of those aggravating early morning regulars at the copy machine.

***Producing materials.*** For anyone who hopes to limit his or her hours during the first year of teaching, the key is clearly sticking to textbooks. Unfortunately, this tactic inevitably clashes with effective instruction. It's not that textbooks aren't thoughtfully written or useful guides, especially to a new teacher. The first year would be impossible if inventing curriculum were added to the pile of responsibilities. But even the most creative textbook does not know your students the way you do, and it doesn't necessarily tap the qualities that make you a great teacher.

My textbook came with all sorts of materials presumably aligned with effective teaching practices. There was even a workbook designed to get students to ask each other questions in pairs (each exercise had an "A" and a "B" version so students would have to query each for information). I used these whenever possible, but I soon had to leave them behind because, inexperienced as I was, I was quickly learning about what emerging adolescents *won't* do—and one of those things was to learn to speak by memorizing grammar charts.

What's more, my textbook was at least five chapters longer than the school year. As a result, most of our Spanish I students know the word for "lettuce" and "onion," but not "fork" or "plate." They can say "gymnasium" and "amusement park" but not "hospital." A teacher who followed the textbook strictly might never teach first-year speakers their 100s, though they would be expected to know "dust the furniture."

These students would be in for a mystifying time in Spanish II, when they encountered these and other common expressions for the first time. The Spanish II students that I taught during my first year did not know "left" and "right" or other critical parts of speech mentioned late in the book. I stuck to the textbook for about a month before I realized we would be parting ways. I wanted to slow down considerably on the grammar while adding more vocabulary.

The result was hours spent at my computer, at school and at home, creating new worksheets, organizers, explanations, and exercises. About halfway through the year I discovered the Quia Web site for teachers, where I could post custom-made exercises (there are many to choose from; but I wound up making my own, and found it saved time compared with searching and tweaking someone else's).

With any luck, this work will pay off next year as I reuse lessons. I may be the only Spanish teacher in York County who is hoping the budget does not allow for the new textbook we've been promised. Incidentally, computerized exercises seem to be well worth the one-time investment in creating them. Not only will many students do things on a keyboard they would never do otherwise (for example, study), but the exercises serve nicely as a preview of quizzes and as "formative assessments," a chance to see what students know before having to tag them with a grade. Once I discovered Quia, I used it to start my tutoring sessions so I could see just what students lacked.

**Grading.** There is no getting around the mountains of grading that come with large class loads. Each weekly quiz results in a stack of 160 papers to be graded and recorded—quickly, of course, so students won't have long to wait for feedback. The biggest challenge may be assigning quizzes on days when I have time to grade them!

I've already learned a few shortcuts that spare the teacher and serve students pretty well:

–   None of the pros I watched in foreign language collect homework for grading. My favorite method has the teacher strolling the room, scanning homework while students are busy with a warm-up. Midway through the year I found that drawing a smiley face or putting a check mark on perfect papers provided enough feedback and motivation for most students. Generally I circled errors and reviewed patterns of mistakes with the whole class. The only grade I recorded was an "H" on the seating chart for those who brought no homework or made a half-hearted effort. Now and then I collected drawings, cartoons, or clippings, culling the best for bulletin boards. I had trouble remembering that homework should never be difficult because it is practice, not learning. Finding a significant number of errors was bad news, because it essentially meant I had sent students home to reinforce bad habits.

–   Have students grade quizzes. This may work better in some subjects than others. The few times I tried it, students found it very satisfying, but I didn't, because their grading was sloppy. It works best for multiple-choice or word-bank quizzes and worst for those that involve spelling. My sister-in-law's method is neatly low-tech: Have students store their pens and pencils. Hand out dark crayons for grading so no one can change answers on the spot.

- Grade "live." In foreign language, it's not only easy but important to collect grades from oral quizzes, skits, dialogues, and scenes. My students seemed to have a blast as I collected test grades during "shopping day," where they ran a miniature shopping mall for paper dolls. For me, it was a chance to measure their mastery without taking home any grading. Question games like "hot seat" (mentioned in chapter two) can also provide a quick grade. On the other hand, oral quizzes at the front of the room generated the most complaints of any activity last year. Some students were visibly shaking when their turns came up.

- Assign graded work with care. I am learning to space out the marvelous projects that exist for foreign language because they require so much grading time. Paired or group work helps cut down the load, of course. I have put off some of my favorite ideas altogether because, multiplied by 100, they simply overwhelm me. Occasionally, I can do these with my smaller Spanish II classes.

- Use rubrics. By now, every teacher is familiar with this way of laying out clear expectations before making assignments. The result is a much higher quality of work, and good grades are certainly easier to cope with than bad ones. Having students create the rubric also helps them remember and get motivated. (For example, "How many sentences do you think an A poster will have?")

***Communicating with families.*** Every teacher seems to have a different attitude about contacting parents. I agree with my first principal that communication with families is as much a part of our job as teaching. If nothing else, it spares me the trauma of meeting with a surprised and anxious mother. But with middle schoolers, there is no question that bad news seldom makes it home with the student. Parents simply won't know they have a problem until it's too late—unless I contact them. I make sure students know I will call and ask them to explain the situation before I do. Half the time this leads to its own solution. Another nice compromise to "turning someone in" is to call home and ask for the student, as a sort of warning. My sister-in-law also reserves one evening a month for "good" calls home. She announces this to her sixth grade class in advance so they can aim for this honor.

My heart went out to a substitute teacher who started working at our school halfway through the year and gave an F to a student without warning the family.

She was soon set straight by the principal. After an especially tough test or during the predictable slump periods last year, I sometimes made dozens of quick phone calls. I noticed that some of our experienced teachers made a regular habit of phoning home during planning periods.

Notes home worked well with some students, but not the most troubled ones. One tiny seventh grader, a year younger than her classmates, routinely forgot her homework but was careful to hand her mother my notes. She needed a parent's reminder to pack her book bag before bed; once I talked to her mother, she got it. Students with bigger problems tended to forget the notes, and after a few days, so did I. It's not easy to remember who is supposed to bring signatures, and I can only imagine how much clout I lost with these students when I didn't demand them.

Parent conferences strike me as a last resort, as opposed to deliberately going to basketball games or concerts in order to shake hands with someone whose child is losing ground. When a parent conference is necessary, it's worth keeping in mind that the very parents you need to speak to most may be the most insecure about speaking to you. One parent told friends she felt "ganged up on" because I had met with her and a guidance counselor. (I had invited the guidance counselor because I was worried about the parent's hostility.) On the other hand, I've heard teachers from other schools talk favorably about student-led conferences.

A word here about which parents to contact when a child is doing poorly: all of them. Early in the year, I could tell—or thought I could—that certain parents expected less of their children than others. They were used to low grades and wouldn't do much to help, I assumed. Why else were they tolerating Cs from the beginning of the year? As a result, I didn't alert these parents soon enough that their children were in trouble. As it turned out, some cared very much and could have done a lot to help. Lesson learned: All parents count, just as all students do.

I also learned the hard way that some parents didn't realize what was at stake. "Dina isn't good at foreign language," her father told me after Christmas break. "She's not very smart. We probably won't put her in Spanish again next year."

"Do you envision Dina going to college?" I asked, maybe a little too bluntly.

"Well, of course," he answered. "Doesn't every parent?"

It turned out he didn't know that nearly all four-year colleges in Virginia require three years of foreign language. Dina, incidentally, was plenty smart enough to learn Spanish or any other subject that motivated her. It was heartbreaking to find out that her own father had told her differently.

There is a flip side to this lesson that is equally important: In speaking to parents, stick to the facts, rather than drawing conclusions. "Johnnie is going to have trouble this year" is offensive and possibly wrong, as opposed to "Johnnie has been missing homework and scoring poorly on tests." You can easily imagine how I learned this lesson!

## Chapter Seven

# How Strict Is Strict Enough?

One of the many traditional bits of wisdom often passed on to new teachers is this: Be strict at the beginning. You can always ease up on discipline, but once the year is underway it's nearly impossible to tighten the reins. This may be great advice, and I agreed with it the first time I heard it. But it's one thing to agree with an idea and another to know how to carry it out. And it is hard to play a role that isn't genuinely you.

In my first year of teaching, discipline simply wasn't that easy or clear. Tony's cheerful but constant wisecracks didn't seem to be a problem, but Tanya's struck me as sassy and challenging. Andy spent a lot of time cracking private jokes with the student next to him. For that matter, so did another half dozen boys in various classes. Was that over the line? What about the way Darien slammed his chair when asked to move to a new seat because he wasn't doing his work? Should Allan be allowed to play with his mechanical pencil every day instead of doing the warm-up? And what of the "clickers," those three or four students in every class who clicked their pens incessantly during tests or quiet instruction?

Some of these minor questions answered themselves, but a few grew into bigger problems. There were times I felt I did as much nagging as teaching in the classes that should have been easiest, the smallest ones. I taught these two groups of Spanish II students—many of whom had done poorly the year before—right after lunch and again at the end of the day. They talked, wisecracked, and, in some cases, simply did not work.

Spanish II marks the beginning of the serious study of Spanish, launching into piles of tenses and other grammar. A 13-year-old who passes this class gets credit for a second-year high school subject. Compared with the easygoing first year of Spanish, there is less room for error by a new teacher, more chance of failure for the student who goofs off or tunes out. Maybe for that reason there was less room for error by me. Every truth in the education books seemed to come to life in my Spanish II classes.

## Save face or save the grade?

One activity that turned into a noisy failure wound up teaching me a great deal about pacing. I had planned what I thought would be an especially fun and effective Spanish II class. This lesson on pronouns had it all: novelty, color, nonlinguistic representation, instant feedback for the students, and ample opportunity for formative assessment for the teacher.

I handed out bags of colored craft sticks that had cost me a summer's afternoon of labeling and cutting. However, students had helped fill the bags, and some were not quite complete. Soon, nearly everyone was yelling out for missing sticks. The novelty of the lesson seemed to destroy what few rules this class normally obeyed. When I finally got everyone quiet and sorted out the missing pieces (not nearly as many as they had thought, once I explained that the sticks had writing on both sides), we were well into our class time. The top students understood right away how to hold up the sticks to represent the missing pronoun in the sentence. Most of the rest were soon lost and aggravated. In the back row, I found two girls trading beauty tips.

The lesson I learned was the old teaching standby of "x+1": Teach one step above what the students already know, and no further. I think this rule is especially important for young adolescents, many of whom would rather save face than save a grade.

Months later, I tried this activity again. This time I used the sticks in Spanish I, where I was more confident of students' behavior. By then, I was also a better teacher—even a few months makes a difference, ask a veteran teacher sometime—and I taught the lesson more slowly, breaking down the learning into smaller steps. This time, the lesson not only worked, but was a hit. Later, I tried it again in Spanish II, with much better success.

Since this experience, I have learned that the "x+1" rule has a corollary: "x" must be roughly the same throughout the class to teach "x+1." In many classes, students simply don't have the same level of knowledge, especially in classes involving the second or third year of a subject. How does anyone teach Spanish III and IV, not to mention V, with all those students handed down from different teachers?

## What's Spanish for "I hate green beans"?

While I struggled with Spanish II, helped by the understanding of the principal and a good bit of counseling from the assistant principal, my Spanish I classes were going fairly smoothly. And why not? The subject couldn't be more basic, and the students were eager and clueless about the 14 verb tenses that stood between them and true fluency. In this class, students learn letters, colors, days of the week, and bits of conversation, such as "Would you like to go to the movies with me Saturday?" Or "I hate green beans. They're disgusting." Taught with plenty of games and skits, first-year Spanish can be as light as kindergarten, and the students seem to love the chance to go back to these playful times. Even when I assigned students to make paper dolls for our shopping project, no one objected, although a few of the results were pierced and tattooed.

I had much more control over these classes, having known the students from their first words in Spanish. If a skill seemed particularly difficult, I simply slowed down and taught it again. Besides the wooden sticks and paper dolls, I used dice, board games, hide and seek, bags of words, whiteboards, poster boards, Web quests, surveys—literally every trick in the books, plus whatever I could steal from other teachers.

Although foreign language is required for Virginia's advanced high school diploma, and is subject to state Standards of Learning, it is not tested by the state. During my entire first year, no one ever pressured me to get to a certain point in the material or questioned my decision to rearrange the order of the text. If anything, my university mentor urged me to slow down and cover substantially less so everyone would get the basics during this critical first year.

With this freedom, my students were soon speaking a very basic but smooth Spanish. On exam days I felt like the audience at a movie theater. My students may have been nervous—I think many of them had never had one-on-one oral tests before—but I was having a blast. Seated at my stool with a clipboard in hand, I happily recorded nearly all top grades as the students surprised me, and maybe themselves, by chatting away easily about their names, ages, and personalities.

The students' success was my pass to continued creative freedom. My university mentor was thrilled with their progress. The administration was happy. The students were starting to see hints of the grammar that makes Spanish one of the hardest subjects in high school, but so far they were nearly all golden.

Nevertheless, even my Spanish I classes had minor problems that got worse during every hot spot on the calendar—the days before spring break, the school dance, summer vacation, big football games.

## Off and running in homeroom

Homeroom was the hardest. Not only was I at my clumsiest, trying out brand new advisory lesson plans, but the students were sleepy and especially mischievous. What's more, I had some of my most challenging personalities in that first class of the day. The warning had come during orientation, when eighth graders roaming the halls had stopped by the homeroom list at my door and laughed at what they read. I followed the advice of the teaching books and pretended I had not heard that Andy, John, Stephen, and Darien were an especially difficult mix of young men to have in one class. I did not want to be prejudiced, right?

Maybe I should have taken the warning and read more about setting routines and laying out class rules. As it turned out, these four students and a couple of others were, if not in control of class, certainly capable of derailing lessons. The "show" started with the morning announcements. An earnest message about the school dress code was easy fodder for Thomas and Dylan, who were soon off and running with their version of color commentary. Even the warm-up activity didn't slow them down. Thomas ignored it, and Dylan, an especially gifted boy, often finished assignments before I could finish handing them out to the rest of class.

Occasionally, I tried making a warm-up puzzle that was outrageously hard, especially for my wisecracking geniuses. It had one of two results: either they finished the puzzle in under a minute, as usual, and returned to searching for something else to do, or they insisted it could not be solved and wouldn't try. The gifted students seemed to have an "on" and "off" setting but no "medium"—a condition I would later learn is common among the brightest middle schoolers.

Besides being fabulously talented, one of my students was the most restless member of the class, regularly standing behind his chair rather than sitting in it. I made sure to call on him when there was an excuse to come to the front of the class. He was one of my volunteers the day I had a line of students at the front of the room demonstrating the verb "tener," which means "to have." By the time his turn came up, he had turned around, logged on to one of the computers behind him, and started surfing the Internet, in full view of the class, but behind my back. Another lesson learned by the teacher.

It wasn't long before 8:55 a.m. felt like the end of the day, not the beginning. First period soon also had consistently lower grades than the other three Spanish I classes. At one point, I took the assistant principal's advice and put my first period class a day behind so that it would be the last to get a lesson, not the first. This way my homeroom students had the benefit of my experience, even if they still had to take a foreign language class at an hour when most youngsters would rather be in bed. The switch got confusing after a while, and I dropped it, but there is no doubt it had helped my students to see me when I'd gained a little experience with the lesson.

On bad mornings—nearly every Monday, for example—I had to summon my experience as a parent and try to remember that the next two classes were a delight and deserved a fresh smile from me. The rest of the day nearly always went better, with my other classes benefiting from the clumsy start.

## The many secrets of classroom management

Because Spanish I is actually a high school credit class in my county, it attracts mostly advanced students with attentive parents. Despite the mischief-makers, my roster was fairly easy to manage. Thank goodness, because I needed a little extra time to learn the classroom control that teachers are magically expected to achieve from the first day.

Surely every new teacher has heard these nuggets of truth:

- Keep a calm voice.
- Have plenty of routines and teach them.
- Use body language rather than words whenever possible.
- Lay out the consequences of misbehavior clearly.
- Get to know the most difficult students.
- Reinforce the rules throughout the year.
- Involve parents.

I hope to make better use of all these strategies next year, but I plan to start with a different golden rule for controlling my class than "start strict." Instead, I will keep "build relationships" as my motto. Building relationships may sound like another of those vague edicts for new teachers, but I'll share my interpretation of it for middle school, which I could not have offered a year ago:

- Show your students they can trust you by treating everyone kindly, not just the easy kids. Joe is more likely to tell the truth about his homework if he sees Keith was treated fairly when he forgot his.

- Be firm without being harsh. This is easier said than done, isn't it? But facing your students without anger is probably the biggest factor in gaining students' trust.

- Eliminate the "parent voice," and talk as you would to another adult. As author Ruby Payne says, some students are used to acting as the adult in their house.

- Respect your students' feelings. While middle schoolers are always looking for a distraction—a bug in the room, a noise outside the door, even a departing school bus—strong emotions really do interfere with their learning. Hear them out if they are upset or excited.

- Listen for the things that matter to teenagers. I don't mean concerts and TV shows, necessarily, nor do I mean trying to be a buddy. Congratulate the poster winner in fourth period and the football captain who kept the team focused. Don't forget to ask about recent injuries; teenagers aren't half as cool as they seem about their bodies.

- Encourage the students who need it most. I had a special friendship with a sixth grader who used a locker near my room when he wasn't being hauled off to the office for his misdeeds. The day he learned to open his own locker—months after everyone else was doing it routinely—I printed him a homemade certificate of congratulations to hang inside. Whatever else happened that day, I knew at least one thing had gone right for him.

- Make sure students know what is expected of them. Routines, rubrics, rules that are reinforced help penetrate the often disorganized brain so students can avoid trouble.

- Analyze common conflicts to eliminate them. Whether homework, or lost pencils, or tardies, it's your policy that needs to change. You don't necessarily have to relax it, but create a routine or an incentive that will help students succeed. By the end of the year, when you have seen students lose everything from pencils to projects, it's tough to follow advice like "take the high ground" and "pick your battles," but the alternative can only bring down your teaching, as well as your students.

- Set easy-to-follow routines. One of the talented sixth grade teachers at my school never has trouble with his students' recording the morning's objective. He starts each class with an egg timer and a reminder of the morning drill. When the sand runs out, students have started their work without questions, debate, or any proclamations that "I didn't know there was a test today!" Silence reigns so that the teacher can begin class.

- Assume the best. Keep your remarks professional and neutral. You can't be sure why Terrance didn't bring his homework, so don't accuse him of ignoring the assignment. Remind him gently of the consequences and make sure he writes down today's assignment.

- Remember, they are still children. Every time I forgot this rule I was eventually sorry. The worse the behavior, the more the student needs a good teacher to guide him through. I knew about the awful statement that got Danny suspended, but I never mentioned it when he came back to school. In this case I also knew a little about what was going on at home. In other cases, I didn't know what led up to misbehavior. There was one student who was especially difficult to love: He seemed to be at the center of every cafeteria fight. Only the head of the guidance department saw him break down in tears as he began failing eighth grade.

- Stop misbehavior early. Looking back, I can see that excess energy was no excuse for students' slapstick behavior in Spanish II. Nor was their reputation for immaturity any reason to get irritated. I would have had a much easier year if I had set limits during the first month, instead of complaining about them all year.

# Chapter Eight

# What Young Adolescents Will Do

Early in the year, nearly all my students were making As. Naturally, I was pleased, but I was also a little worried. Did this mean my tests were too easy? Were my students really learning, or was I fooling myself (and misleading them)? What would happen when they moved on to another, harder teacher? I knew some of my students were much weaker than others, and it seemed wrong for all of them to be making the same grade.

By the end of the year I knew I needn't have worried. There were enough Ds, unfortunately, to allay any fears I had that my grading was too easy. The slower students had sunk to lower grades. The quicker ones had kept their high grades. While the very brightest couldn't be set apart—their 97s and 98s looked the same on a report card as the more modest 92s and 94s—just about everyone else was in the "proper" place.

Instead of feeling better, I was suddenly sad. Why hadn't I reached those slower students? If most students earned grades in keeping with their abilities, that meant I hadn't taught them to be better learners, didn't it? What's more, those early high grades, which turned out to be natural in the easy first weeks, had allowed all but one student to move on to Spanish II. Most of them took their skills, or lack of skills, on to high school teachers who would have to deal with the disparity. About 20 were young enough to enroll in Spanish II with me.

# Teach what they need to learn

As I scanned my roster for this advanced class, I realized I had a class half filled with students who could barely pass a grammar quiz. Spanish II is rather monstrous, grammatically, tackling three tenses and many of the subtler problems of Spanish grammar. How was I going to reach students who had struggled with Spanish I?

Suddenly, I repented of my easygoing, active classes. If I had been tougher, more by the book, I would have flunked a few students, discouraged the ones too immature for high school credit, and had an easier roster for Spanish II. Looking ahead to my second year of middle school teaching, I promised myself and the guidance department I would give some tough tests early on to show these students they needed to retake Spanish I. What's more, I made it clear to these unfortunate students that their performance was not good enough. They were doing poorly, I told them; and the coming year was very hard.

My college mentor was appalled. No, she did not agree that I should drive these students out, and not at all did she approve of my tough tone in class. "Take them where they're at," she told me, for at least the sixth time that year.

How had I forgotten so quickly? Certainly, I knew—I had even preached with the fervor of a new teacher—that anxiety is bad for learning. Yet I had put these students, the very ones I had hoped most to reach at the beginning of the year, outside my normal expectations. They were slower; they studied less; they were less organized. They seemed not to be worth my effort. But of course, they were worth the most effort of all. At 13, a child who doesn't know how to study is a child in need of extra lessons—lessons in how to keep his notebook organized, how to set goals, and most of all, how to believe he can learn.

Working with young adolescents, I now see, means following their lead. Are they restless? Get them out of their chairs. Are they self-centered? Give them a pencil and the words to write about themselves. Are they playful and goofy? Give them a game. Are they out of bounds? Set some limits.

I will long remember the day the eighth graders were out on a field trip and my few seventh graders had the class to themselves. We couldn't move ahead, because these students were among the most difficult to manage when they got bored. Instead, we played games. I insisted these be in Spanish but did not try to cover any special material. One after the other, these 11- and 12-year-olds vied for the chance to come to the front of the room and get a "secret identity" hung around their necks, a card lying on their backs so they couldn't see it. They had to ask questions in Spanish before guessing who they were. If a girl became Santa Claus or a boy became Jennifer Lopez, so much the better. They shrieked and laughed, and by the next day knew how to form questions with the irregular verb "ser" as well as any eighth grader. So much for my worry that seventh graders were too young to learn Spanish grammar.

On the best days, teaching middle school feels to me like some fast-paced sport where the balance is always shifting, like surfing or downhill skiing. I do best on the days when I stay light on my feet and change to match the terrain—to match the needs of my students. There is no point in arguing with the people who face me at the morning bell. A skier might as well blame gravity for a fall.

Which brings me back to the story of Jeremy, who met me at the door without an answer after many lessons on conjugating Spanish verbs. After a day or two, I came back to class with an idea.

"It's story time," I announced and, unbelievably, faces perked up. "Once upon a time, there was a boy who…"

The students listened in more or less rapt attention as I told the story of a 13-year-old named Juan, eager to ask out a beautiful girl named Juanita. Instead, he winds up inviting her grandmother to the movies. It's all because he doesn't conjugate the verb correctly, and Juanita's grandmother misunderstands him. See the dangers of ignoring conjugation?

Not everyone took the hint, despite our new classroom slogan, which became, "You asked out the grandmother!" But Jeremy, who was on his second year of Spanish I, finished with a high A.

In June, I asked him how he went from Cs and Ds to nearly perfect grades.

"Once I got conjugation, it was easy," he said, with a shrug.

Once he got conjugation, it was easy. It didn't escape me that I had nothing to do with it, at least from Jeremy's point of view. Well, that's okay. There are many lessons to be learned in the first year of teaching, and I had just learned a big one. I had learned that I just might survive my first year of middle school. I just needed to let students like Jeremy teach me how to do my job.

# Postscript

Two years have passed since I waited for my first middle school students to come through the door at Yorktown Middle School. My second year was a bit easier, naturally, but it was no less a wild ride.

In year two, I got a new principal, 150 new students, and a new schedule. (Spanish II, with its lineup of difficult verbs, was set for the last period of the day—interrupted routinely by dismissals for doctor visits, tornado drills, concerts, ball games, and even team and choir practices.) Halfway through the year we moved to trailers on the high school lawn to await renovations to our school. The makeshift campus set the tone for many students who seemed to view school as a temporary arrangement. Eventually the principal banned all bathroom breaks until the last 10 minutes of class, which cut down on the sidewalk social visits and cell phone calls from toilet stalls; but tardies remained a problem all year. One day in June, nearly half my last class walked in late.

Changes outside our control affected school, too. Besides the ongoing Iraq War, the Virginia Tech shootings took place in May, which affected many more students than the few who blamed it for their missing work. A sidewalk shooting in a nearby neighborhood hurt one of the school's former students, to the horror and excitement of her friends, while the sudden death of a parent cost another child his father.

In my own class, the previous year's skateboarder with an attitude problem was gone, and so were many of my restless but gifted boys. In their place were a surprising number of students with attention deficit disorder, problems identified only after I contacted families about their children's having trouble focusing in class. I also had a batch of enormously smart girls, fresh from summer growth spurts that burdened a few of them with depression. Two students never emerged from the bangs that hung over half their faces, and many more had trouble coming out from behind their anime books. Several students I simply couldn't reach the first year came back the second year, giving me another chance (with mixed results).

The second year's students were—if anything—more typical of their generation than my first year's. Quick, witty, and more electronically connected than ever, most of them were juggling school, sports, and cell phones with impressive skill, though they had trouble keeping track of old-fashioned tools like library books and study guides. Nearly half seemed to be going home to two sets of parents, and I often heard the excuse "the book was at my Dad's house" when homework was missing.

Students had popular Spanish songs on their iPods before I could introduce them in class. With the ever present cell phones, I learned it was not enough to ban a student from leaving the classroom to call home for forgotten work. He simply sent his mother a text message from the phone under his desk. Poker was the favorite time-filler among boys whenever my lesson plans left them feeling too free. The same students who couldn't find their vocabulary cards could often produce a deck of playing cards and even chips! During the last month of class, I confiscated a metal case containing a complete Texas hold 'em poker set.

Maybe I simply noticed it more, but this batch of students seemed to have a harder time with the basic requirements of school. The extra pencils disappeared sooner; there were more nameless notebooks in the lost-and-found bin in June. During the last week of school, something like half of my students still hadn't handed in the collection of vocabulary cards I required. A dozen more were never able to show me the grammar folder everyone else had created. Late in the year, I finally appealed to the baseball coach to get one of my more intelligent eighth graders to buy the spiral notebook I required. ("Why should I?" the ballplayer had asked, referring to his ability to hold a B average without it.) A student who had begun struggling in Spanish II asked, in all sincerity, why I would expect her to take notes in class. "It's not like I'm flunking," she said. "Not yet!" I fumed.

Another teacher summed it up early in the year: This group was especially intelligent, he said, and especially uninterested in schoolwork. Clearly, if teaching were going to get any easier for me, it wouldn't be thanks to the task at hand.

## Two steps forward, one step back?

Meanwhile, I had made some changes of my own—many more routines, a few more rules, and a touch more reality in the lessons. My classes searched the Internet for Mayan ruins and sampled Hispanic foods. With modeling-clay people and digital cameras we made hilarious and tragic PowerPoint presentations for our "injury" unit. Our homemade piñatas nearly did in the school's old plumbing, but served as a neat little public service project, becoming the centerpiece of a fiesta in a special needs classroom. At year's end, I braved a small field trip, bypassing the popular Mexican restaurants to take my most unruly class to a Puerto Rican café and dance club. (The students did beautifully and ate heartily. Next year we'll add a salsa lesson.)

My Web site had pictures during the second year and many more online games. It also featured the winners of a poster contest, created by begging prizes from catalog companies and copying the Foreign Language Association of Virginia. It drew only three entries but surprised everyone by generating the state winner.

During this second year, I also surprised myself by realizing that I could get bored with lessons, even successful ones, and would probably always have to change a few of my plans just to stay interested.

For the first time, I required notebooks and graded them, but not often enough, as I would learn by year's end. I also collected students' homemade vocabulary cards every semester, solving one problem (index cards littering the hallways) and causing another one (zeros for those who wouldn't do the work). I picked up the pace in Spanish I and started grammar earlier, losing hardly anyone along the way—a real victory.

Spanish II was no victory, however, as I continued to struggle both for control of the room and for lesson plans that would reach a mix of gifted and apathetic students. Frustrated with Spanish II and a handful of Spanish I students, I lost my temper on many days. For the second year in a row, I had especially aggravating relationships with a few repeat offenders. I know there were days when certain students left my class feeling worse than when they arrived. In short, I had much to learn.

Reading my own advice in the preceding pages, I can only say that being a new teacher is not much different from being a middle schooler: We may know right from wrong, but we can't always put it into practice. Worse still, I actually did some things better the first year than the second. I think I was more optimistic and spontaneous that first year, as I dared to do outrageous things simply because I didn't know they couldn't be done.

## The best years?

In August, I began what many administrators consider the best years of most teaching careers, years three to five—that period when a person has enough experience to avoid the big mistakes but still has plenty of energy and enthusiasm.

I am certainly a better teacher than in my first few months. At least I can find my whiteboard markers and lesson plans most days. I have already had the thrilling experience of running into an old student unexpectedly and hearing that I was "the best Spanish teacher" she's *ever* had (a boost even if she is only 13). I have my file of sweet notes from students and parents, and a goofy certificate from the administration for "innovative teaching."

What would that certificate say if it were written by some of my problem students? Surely not "innovative." Maybe "most aggravating," or "lectures too much." "I don't like you!" a boy finally yelled at me after days of confrontation over missing work and blurted wisecracks. At the time I thought he could have said something worse, but now I'm not sure.

I have friends in teaching who are loved by their students, good and bad. They may be strict, or they may use a wry humor, but they can deflect the problems of this age group without getting personal about it. Their students have no doubt that they care. When they get tired, they may retire, but I don't think they will ever burn out. Before I retire, I'd like to be like them.

# Want to Learn More?

Blaz, D. (1999). *Foreign language teacher's guide to active learning.* Larchmont, NY: Eye on Education.

National Middle School Association. (2003). *This we believe: Successful schools for young adolescents.* Westerville, OH: Author.

Payne, R. (1996). *A framework for understanding poverty.* Highlands, TX: aha! Process.

Wong, H., & Wong, R. (2004). *The first days of school: How to be an effective teacher.* Mountain View, CA: Harry K. Wong.

http://www.quia.com/
See the Instructor Zone to create activities, quizzes, games, Web pages, surveys, and more on Quia Web.

# About National Middle School Association

Since 1973, National Middle School Association (NMSA) has been the voice for those committed to the education and well-being of young adolescents and is the only national association dedicated exclusively to middle grades youth.

NMSA's more than 30,000 members are principals, teachers, central office personnel, professors, college students, parents, community leaders, and educational consultants in the United States, Canada, and 46 other countries. A major advocacy of NMSA's is the recognition of October as Month of the Young Adolescent. This celebration engages a wide range of organizations to help schools, families, and communities celebrate and honor young adolescents for their contributions to society.

NMSA offers publications, professional development services, and events for middle level educators seeking to improve the education and overall development of 10- to 15-year-olds. In addition to the highly acclaimed *Middle School Journal*, *Middle Ground* magazine, and *Research in Middle Level Education Online*, we publish over 100 books on every facet of middle level education. Our landmark position paper, *This We Believe: Successful Schools for Young Adolescents*, is recognized as the premier statement outlining the vision of middle level education.

Membership is open to anyone committed to the education of young adolescents. Visit www.nmsa.org or call 1-800-528-NMSA for more information.